ADVENTURE TIME™

THIS ANNUAL BELONGS TO:

Name: ~~cAmeroF~~ Cameron _____

Address: _____

_____

EDITORIAL Editor: David Leach • **Designer**: Donna Askem • Thanks to Jake Devine

TITAN COMICS Senior Comics Editor: Martin Eden • **Production Supervisors** Jackie Flock, Maria Pearson • **Production Assistant** Peter James • **Art Director** Oz Browne
Studio Manager Emma Smith • **Circulation Manager** Steve Tothill • **Marketing Manager** Ricky Claydon • **Marketing Assistant** Jaleesa Lynsdale • **Advertising Manager**
Michelle Fairlamb • **Publishing Manager** Darryl Tothill • **Publishing Director** Chris Teather • **Operations Director** Leigh Baulch • **Executive Director** Vivian Cheung •
Publisher Nick Landau

ADVENTURE TIME Annual 2015

ISBN: 9781782760245

Published by Titan Comics, a division of Titan Publishing Group Ltd., 144 Southwark St., London, SE1 0UP.
ADVENTURE TIME, CARTOON NETWORK, the logos, and all related characters and elements are trademarks of and © Cartoon Network. (S14) All rights reserved. All characters,
events and institutions depicted herein are fictional. Any similarity between any of the names, characters, persons, events and/or institutions in this publication to actual names,
characters, and persons, whether living or dead and/or institutions are unintended and purely coincidental.

A CIP catalogue record for this title is available from the British Library.

Printed in Italy.

This edition first published: August 2014

CONTENTS

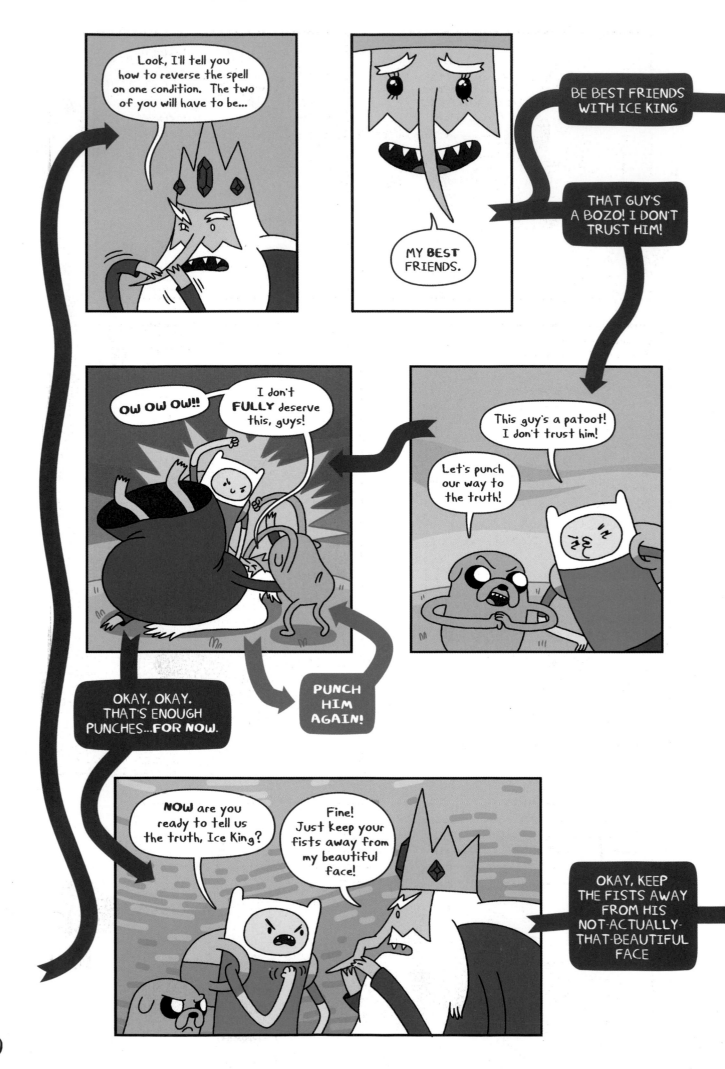

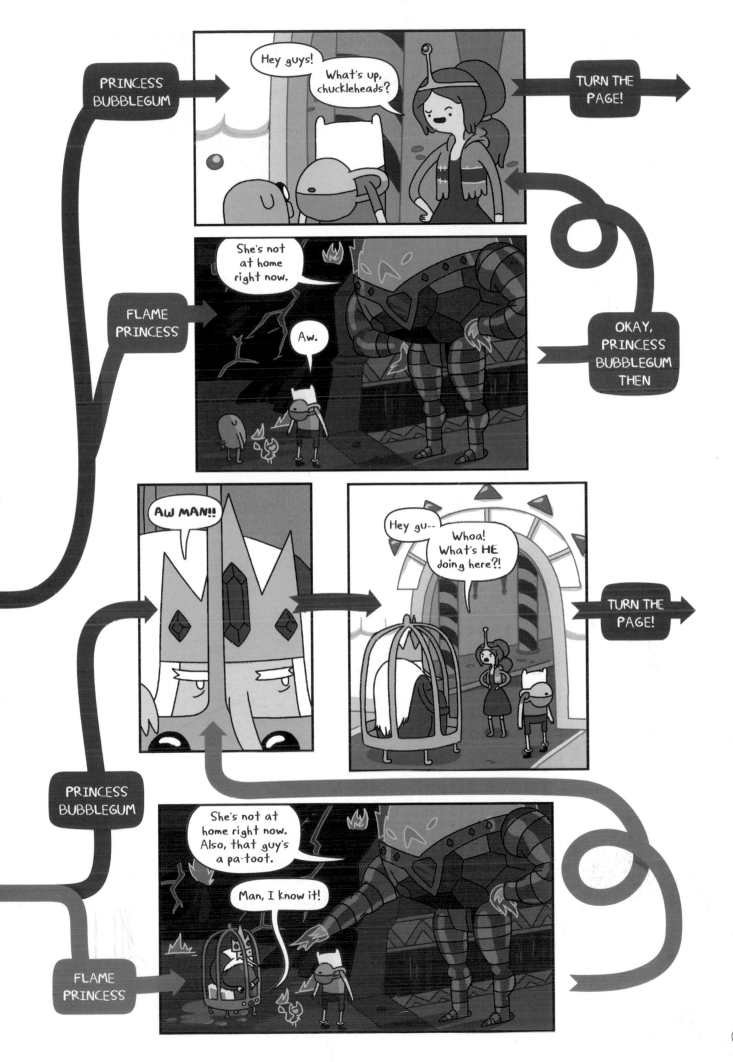

TURN THE PAGE!

SHOOT BUBBLEGUM DOWN! THAT'LL NEVER WORK

EXPLORE PRINCESS BUBBLEGUM'S ROYAL TOOT PLAN

TURN THE PAGE!

TURN THE PAGE!

TURN THE PAGE!

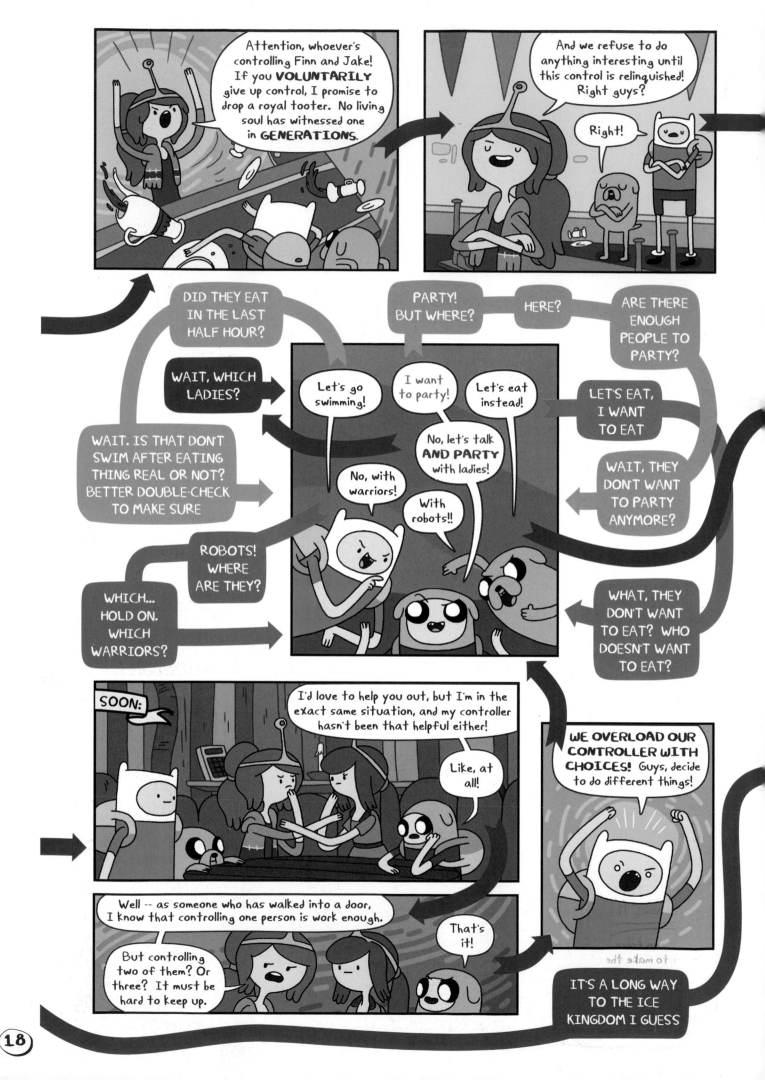

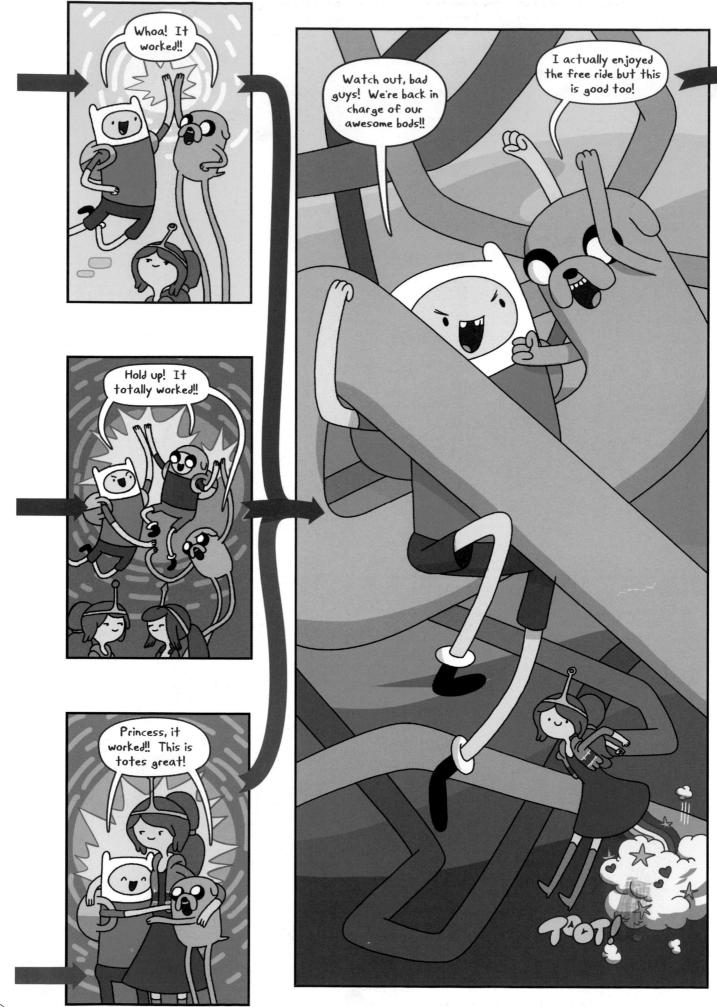

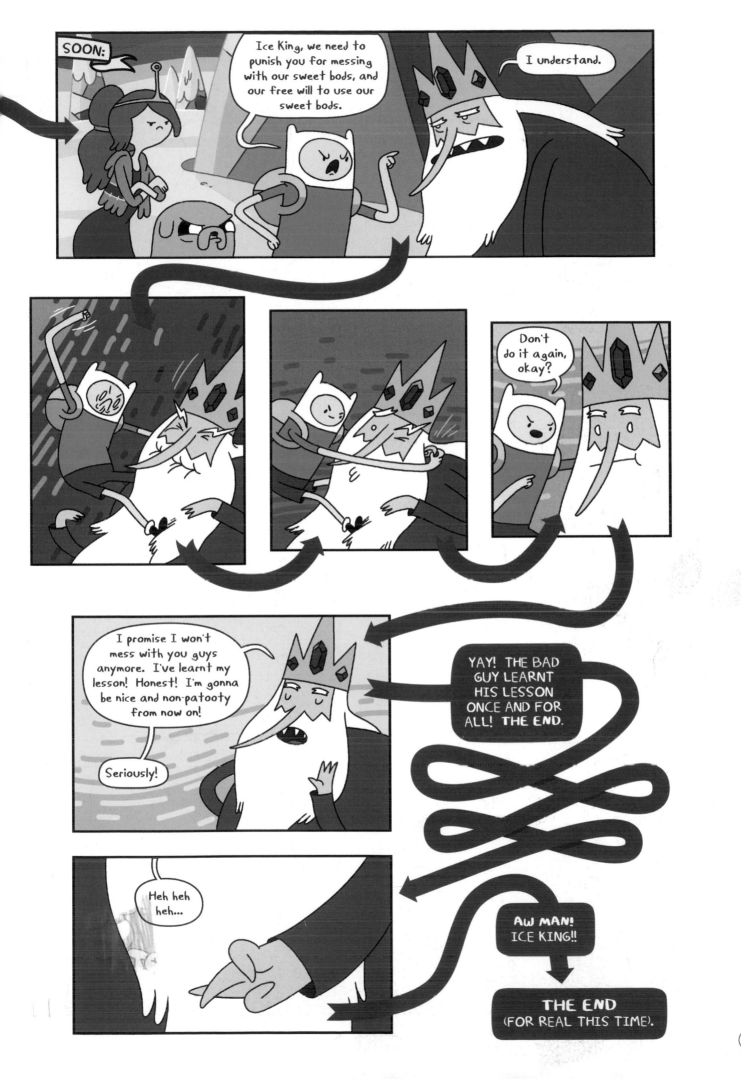

PUZZLE TIME

ICE KING'S CHRISTMAS CAPERS

Ice King is mad with glee and wants to celebrate Christmas with his awesome bros and fav princesses! Help him impress them with these righteous puzzles made for fistfuls of frozen fun.

Ooh, the guys are so gonna love this!

HOLLY JOLLY FOLLY

Take a gander at these awesome Ooo facts. Bet you can't tell the totes fake ones from the righteous truth!

1. Finn lost his left arm.

2. Princess Bubblegum created Lemonhope.

3. Jake is the father of six half-dog/half-rainicorn puppies.

4. Ice King's real name is Peter Simokov.

5. Marceline is allergic to the colour red.

Hehe! I know the answers.

GUNTER HUNTER

Can you find Ice King's fav Gunter before all the radical festivities start?

SCALING THE ICE KINGDOM

Finn and Jake need to get to the Ice King and save the princesses from his boring stories... again! Help them scale the mountain by filling in the gaps so each pair adds up to the numbers above.

17
7

8	120	110

WINTER WORDSEARCH

Buried in this righteous grid are 10 words that are all connected. When you've found them all, rearrange the highlighted letters to discover the link.

J	U	S	B	R	E	L	M	A	A	L	K	O
I	C	I	E	U	H	H	X	Y	C	R	A	M
K	F	M	T	B	U	W	A	X	O	R	V	M
D	I	O	T	V	G	I	I	M	S	F	M	I
X	V	N	Y	P	V	E	N	Z	B	J	C	D
R	G	P	M	H	V	A	K	U	A	O	C	Z
F	W	E	J	H	Z	N	L	A	E	R	U	E
B	J	T	N	B	T	N	B	K	C	S	D	Z
P	C	R	O	W	N	O	I	B	W	M	A	J
S	N	I	R	J	T	I	Z	A	E	U	P	I
H	J	K	D	T	G	F	R	Q	M	R	W	Z
Y	W	O	I	M	I	Y	X	Y	P	D	Y	U
Z	I	V	G	U	N	T	E	R	T	H	S	X

SIMON PETRIKOV   CROWN
BETTY   HAMBO
GUNTER   WIZARD
FIONNA   DRUMS
MARCY   CAKE

BMO-COP

BMO has been put in charge of security for the algebraic Christmas party. Identify these creepy characters so they don't knock the math vibes.

If they try to crash the party, BMO will kick them in the buns!

SNOW DOTS

Join up the dots to find out who's hiding here?

23

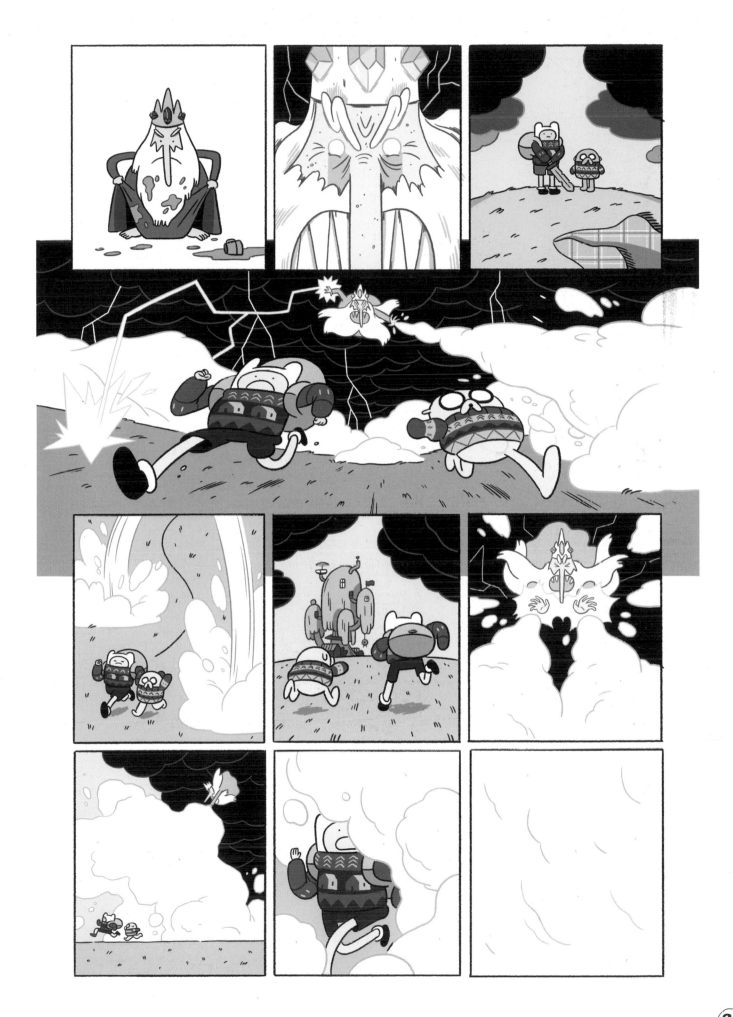

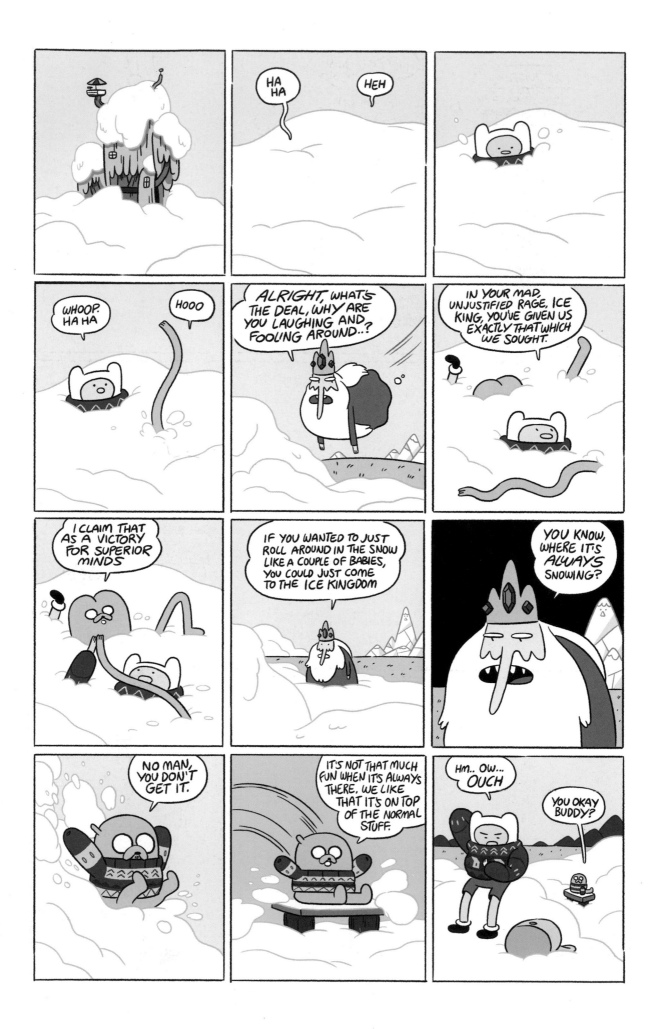

BRAIN STUFF TESTER

ROUND 1: GENERAL KNOWLEDGE

Below are 12 simple questions designed to trick and test you. See how many you can get right, but be careful because they might not be as easy as they seem...

Take the test, then check your score.

1 If you are running in a race and overtake the person in second place, what position are you in now?

2ⁿᵈ place

2 What do cows drink?

Water

3 How many birthdays does the average person have?

4 Where in the world do the biggest potatoes grow?

5 In the Bigger family, who is the biggest and why? Mr. Bigger, Mrs Bigger or their baby?

6 Brian's mother had four children. The first was called April, the second May and the third she called June. But what was the name of her fourth child?

SO, HOW DID OOO DO?

Wak! Wak, wak, wak!

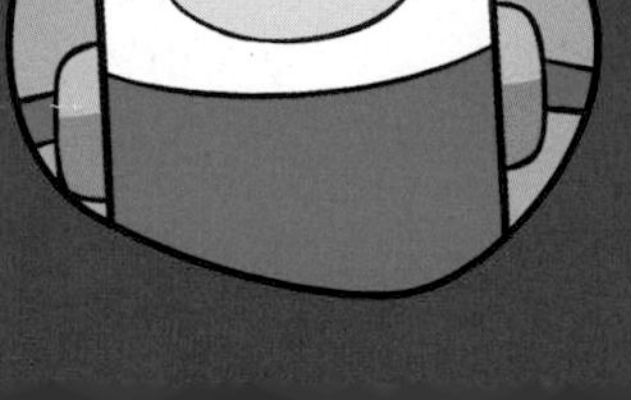

Poor old Gunter only scored 3, but I got him beat with 6 points! I gots brains and moves! So, what did you get, Jake?

ROUND 2: MATH PROBLEMS

1 If you have four grapefruits in one hand and three watermelons in the other, what do you have?

2 How many seconds does a regular year have?

3 If two is company and three is a crowd, what are four and five?

4 Some months of the year have 31 days, but how many have 28?

5 You are driving a bus... At the first stop 14 people get on, at the second three get on, at the third stop 10 people get on, and at the last stop 22 people get on. What was the name of the bus driver?

6 It takes four men three hours to build a wall. How long does it take three men to build the same wall?

Don't forget to turn to page 68 for the answers!

You did well, mighty Adventurer, but not as good as me! I scored 9! Looks like I still got you beat, bro!

Well, sorry to burst your bubble guys, but I scored a perfect 12! Looks like I got you both whupped!

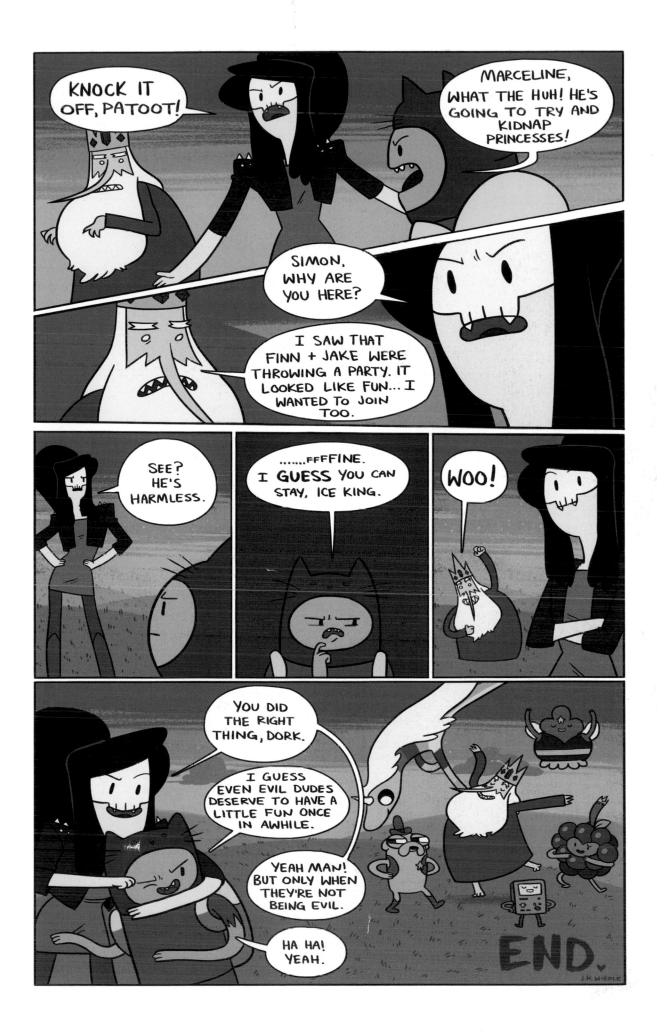

PUZZLE TIME

FINN AND JAKE'S SIZZLING SUMMER PUZZLERS!

A righteous summer blowout is in full swing, but in the Land of Ooo adventure is only around the corner for our bro-tastic heroes!

THROUGH THE FIRE AND FLAMES

Lead Flame Princess away from the clutches of her evil father and his prison safely to her trusted friend Cinnamon Bun.

A

B

C

DOUBLE TROUBLE

Oh Glob, Flame King's escaped his candle cage and is trying to ruin the fun! Spot the decoy's five differences and put the fiery fiend back in his place.

FINDING EVERYTHING

Help Jake create the most mathematical food in the history of Ooo! Across the page are 10 different ingredients for the Everything Burrito - can you find them all?

Grob, I'm super excited for this!

You got math cooking skills, brah.

FOODOKU

Tree Trunks is happily arranging the food to look stupendously splendid for all the partygoers. Help her out by placing each food item so that it appears once in each row and column.

Oh my, these are the best apple pies I've ever made, if I do say so myself.

BILLY'S OCEAN

Finn must fight his way through his fear of the ocean to reach Billy. Help guide him on his quest of courage and avoid the Fear Feaster.

CANDY SLUSH

Dude! The candy people have gone totally mush in the heat. Sort them out by naming all four of them.

PUZZLE TIME

MARCELINE'S FANG-TASTIC BRAIN-CRUNCHERS

Eating red is heavy business and you've got to stay sharp, especially if you have to match wits with the likes of P-bubs. Assist the Vampire Queen with these chillingly math puzzles.

CHORD OF CALAMITY!

Marceline has created a new musical note that has split the very fabric of space and time! Can you help her to piece back the universe before anyone notices?

A B C D E F G H

OVER DUB

The deep bass notes of Marceline's ax guitar have created overdubbed versions of herself. Can you match up the pairs to find the real Marceline?

A B C D E

FRAN-KING-STEIN'S MONSTER

Shmowzow! Ice King's recreated Princess Monster Wife and it's terrifying the penguins. Match the body parts to the correct Princesses to send them back where they belong.

A ← B ← C ↓ D ← E → F ↑ G

Waak Wak Waaaakk!!

RUBY, RUBY, RUBY, RUBY!

Marceline's getting hungry for red and she's totes going banaynay! Hurry and collect all nine rubies before she hits the roof!

QUIZ TIME!

1 Which evil creature was turned into a baby?

a. The Lich
b. Hunson Abadeer
c. Flame King

2 Who became captain of the Banana Guards?

a. Finn
b. Root Beer Guy
c. Peppermint Butler

3 Which demon's blood was used to make the demon sword?

a. Death
b. Marceline
c. Kee Oth

4 How many clones of James were there?

a. 10
b. 25
c. 30

MAGIC MAN-IA!

Magic Man's up to his old tricks and has trapped Finn and Jake in a dungeon. Follow the maze to lead them out, but watch out for all the traps and monsters!

51

FIVE MINUTES EARLIER:

Would you pass the tea, Ghost Princess 2?

Oh um it would be my pleasure, Princess Bubblegum! And please, call me "Spookette."

Spookette! What a perfectly excellent name!

I'm so glad the Princess Tea Party happened during summer this year. It's so hard to find a nice winter dress!

I made this hat out of a breakfast taquito!

It's delightful!

You asked me to make sure you didn't break your "no sammiches" diet!

Past Me was dumb to go on that diet! Past Me didn't remember how tasty sammiches are!

So I was all, MELISSA, don't even talk to me like you know my business, 'cause I know you don't know! And I know you know I know you don't know!

Wow, how--um... interesting!

I don't know why she even says that junk! Save it for your dumb diary, you know?

Uh... yes?

SQUEEZ-E-MART

Oh my glob, Hot Dog Princess, you'll love this: do you have ANY IDEA what the very next thing she said to me was?

Nope.

NOTHING!

She hung up her lumping phone on me!

She didn't even say "Oh wow, peace out LSP, you know I gotta go be jealous of your mad lumps now!" Can you even BELIEVE HER?

Wow.

I swear to glob, I love her, but I cannot lumpin' stand her sometimes. You know how it's like you're friends, but you kinda can't stand to be around them sometimes because they're SO LUMPIN' ANNOYING??

Uhh...

SQUEEZ-E-MART

I know just the feeling, ladies!

Everything's going so well! Should we warn the princesses about what we saw on the previous page? Naw, it's probably... it's probably fine. Right?

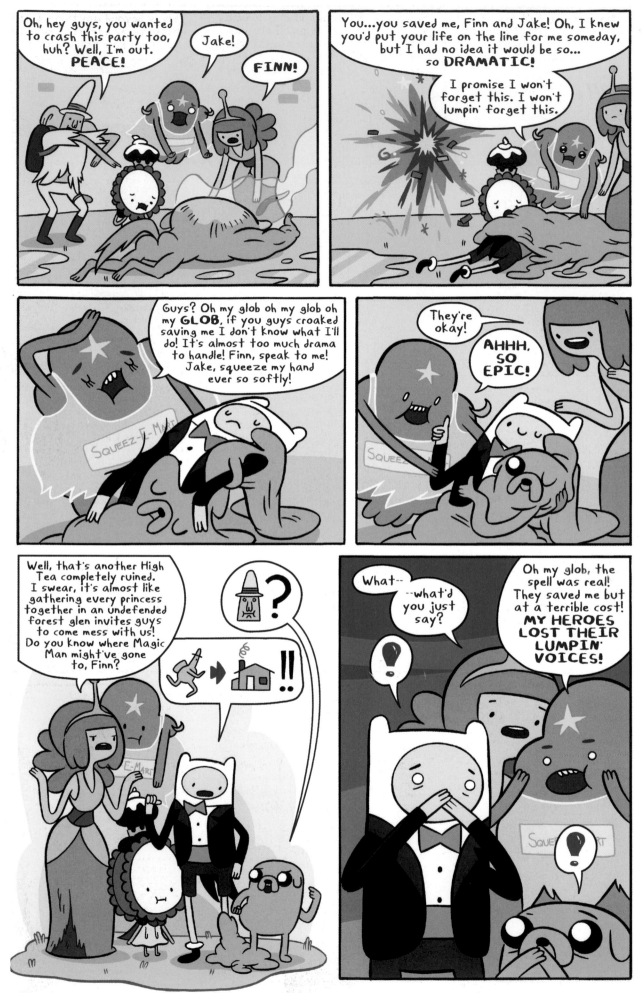

I don't know why you're reading this down here when such nutty things are happening up above.
I don't know what's going to happen! I find out at the same time you do!

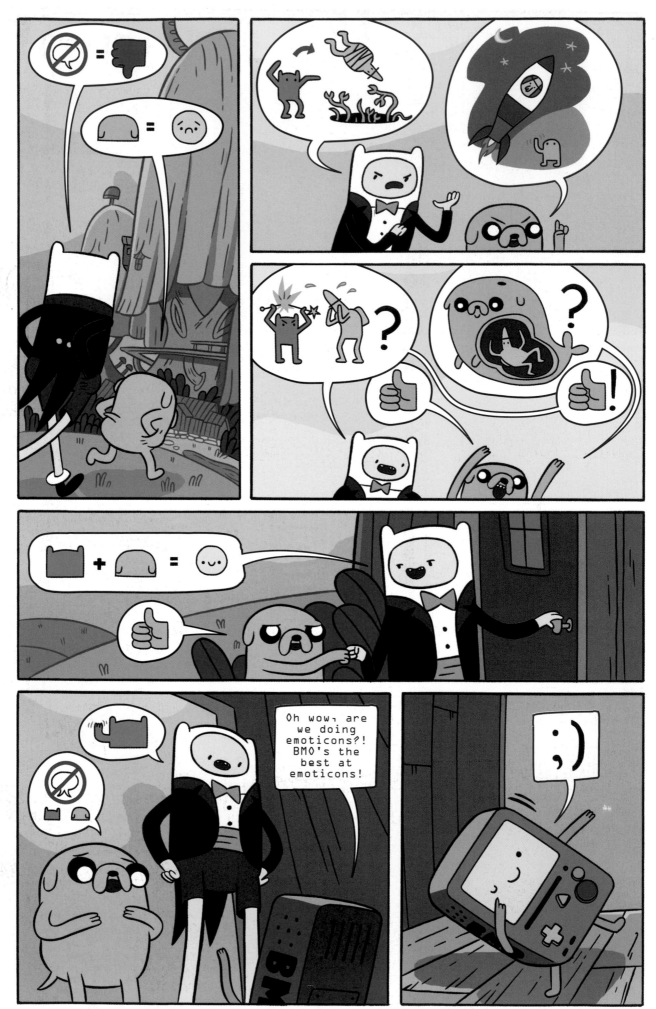

Oh wow, are we doing emoticons?! BMO's the best at emoticons!

:)

Sandwiches do not work that way BMO. I've tried. Oh how I've tried.

Okay, so here's the plan: every princess will use her skillset to lay a separate trap outside Magic Man's house, all to be sprung simultaneously. For example, mine will be science-themed.

Mine will be a pit full of water!

Mine will be a mouth full of awful lampreys!

Then we knock on his door! When he comes out he's gonna get covered in a big ol' lumpload of traps!

Then you demand he give you your voice back, and if he doesn't, we'll just ki—

I can hear you, you know!

SQUEEZ-E-MART

What kind of plan was it to discuss the plan outside my house? I'm magic, man! And I'm keeping Finn and Jake's voices forever now!

I'm gonna sell them to bad guys so they can make prank phone calls with 'em!

Finn and Jake will get in trouble because people will think it was them!

We won't let that happen, guys, I promise. We'll come up with a new plan, and this time we **WON'T** discuss it in earshot of the bad guy. By the way, thanks for the **REAL GREAT IDEA** you had, Let's All Discuss Our Plans In Front Of The Bad Guy Princess!

I'm sorry!

Also my name's Samantha

Oh my glob you guys I think I've got it! I seriously think I've got it!

Everyone let's go away from this guy so I can tell you my lumpin' plan in private!

?

Okay! Don't come back ever, okay? Stay away now!

THE ANSWERS

PG 22. ICE KING'S CHRISTMAS CAPERS

HOLLY JOLLY FOLLY:
They are all false! 1. Finn lost his right arm.
2. Lemongrab created Lemonhope. 3. Jake has five kids,
Jake Jnr, Charlie, TV, Viola and Kim Kil Whan.
4. Ice King's first name is Simon.
5. Marceline needs the colour red to live!

SCALING THE ICE KINGDOM:
10, 2, 5 are the missing numbers.

BMO-COP:
A=The Lich, B=Swamp Monster, C=King Worm,
D= Magic Man, E=The Door Lord.

WINTER WORDSEARCH:
The highlighted letters spell Ice King

SNOW DOTS:
It's Finn and Jake!

PG 32. BRAIN TESTER

GENERAL KNOWLEDGE:
1. You are in second place.
2. Cows drink water.
3. One. The day you are born.
4. Underground.
5. The baby, because she's a little bigger.
6. Brian is the name of the fourth child.

MATH SOLUTIONS:
1. Big Hands.
2. There are 12 seconds in a year. 2nd of
Jan, 2nd of Feb, 2nd of March etc.
3. 4 + 5 = Nine.
4. All 12 months have 28 days.
5. Whatever is the name of the person doing
this quiz. 'You are the bus driver.'
6. There's no need. Four men have already
built it.

PG 40. FINN AND JAKE'S SIZZLING SUMMER PUZZLERS!

THROUGH THE FIRE AND FLAMES:
Route B.

DOUBLE TROUBLE :
1. The Flame King's hair is a different
colour, 2. He's smiling, 3. There's an extra
gem on his armour, 4. One of the bands on
his armour is a different colour. 5. The gem
on the flame on his head is missing.

BILLY'S OCEAN

FOODOKU

CANDY SLUSH:
Peppermint Butler,
Cinnamon Bun, Starchie
and Mr. Cupcake.

PG 50. MARCELINE'S FANG-TASTIC BRAIN-CRUNCHERS!

CHORD OF CALAMITY:

OVER DUB:
The real Marceline is D.

QUIZ TIME!:
1. a. The Lich, 2. b. Root Beer Guy,
3. c. Kee Oth, 4. b. 25.

FRAN-KING-STEIN'S MONSTER:
A. Princess Bubblegum.
B. LSP.
C. Wildberry Princess.
D. Hot Dog Princess.
E. Turtle Princess.
F. Muscle Princess.
G. Skeleton Princess.

MAGIC MAN-IA

Did you find me?
I was on pages 12,
23, 25, 36, 41, 46,
62 and 69.